# Albania

## Travel Guide
## 2024

Your Ultimate Travel Companion For
2024 And Beyond

### Monica Friend

***Copyrighted Material***

**Copyright©Monica Friend2023**
**All right reserved.**

***Copyrighted Material***

# Content

Introduction
About Albania
   History and Culture
   Geography and Climate
   Getting There
   Getting Around
Planning Your Trip
   When to visit
   Visa and Passport Requirements
   Things to pack
   Tips for staying safe
Exploring Albania
   Tirana
   Berat and Gjirokastra
   Butrint
   The Majestic Albanian Alps
   The Albanian Riviera
Food And Drinks
   Traditional Albanian cuisine
   Recommend Restaurant
Best Places to Visit
Accommodation

***Copyrighted Material***

Practical Information
    Exploring the Local Language
    Tips for Travelers
    Shopping
    Emergency
Your 5 Days Itinerary
Conclusion

# Map

# Introduction

Tucked away in the heart of the Balkans, Albania reveals itself as a hidden treasure for travelers seeking an untouched European adventure. My recent trip to this captivating country left a lasting impression on my travel memories. Albania's rich history, stunning landscapes, and friendly hospitality make it a must-see destination for those looking to explore a unique side of Europe.

My journey started in Tirana, Albania's lively capital city. Despite its size, Tirana exudes a vibrant atmosphere with its bustling cafes, colorful buildings, and an unmistakable sense of optimism. I delved into the city's history by visiting landmarks like the Et'hem Bey Mosque and the National Historical Museum, gaining insights into Albania's tumultuous past and its remarkable path to independence. The youthful spirit of the city comes alive in the Blloku district, once reserved for Communist elites and now a trendy area filled with shops, bars, and restaurants.

Continuing my exploration southward, I encountered some of the most awe-inspiring natural beauty I've ever witnessed along the

Albanian Riviera. Its unspoiled beaches and crystal-clear waters left me enchanted. From the charming coastal town of Himara to the hidden gem of Dhermi, each spot along the Riviera had its unique charm and offered a chance to unwind in peaceful surroundings. One of the highlights was hiking through Llogara Pass, which rewarded me with breathtaking views of the Ionian Sea and lush mountains.

What truly distinguishes Albania is the warmth of its people. Albanians are incredibly welcoming and proud of their culture. I had the privilege of sharing traditional Albanian meals with locals in remote villages, savoring homemade dishes like qofte (meatballs) and byrek (savory pastries) while enjoying folk music. These encounters deepened my appreciation for the rich tapestry of Albanian culture.

My journey through Albania was an exceptional experience that surpassed all expectations. From the lively streets of Tirana to the pristine beaches of the Albanian Riviera and the genuine hospitality of its people, Albania offers a unique and unforgettable travel experience. This hidden gem of Europe is a destination not to be missed by any avid traveler seeking an authentic and off-the-beaten-path adventure. Albania has firmly etched itself into my heart, and I eagerly anticipate returning to explore more of its unspoiled beauty and rich heritage.

# About Albania

## History and Culture

Albania, situated in southern Europe on the Balkan Peninsula, graces the western coast of the Strait of Otranto, the gateway to the Adriatic Sea. The vibrant capital is Tirana (Tiranë).

Albanians, often self-identified as "shqiptarë," which might mean "sons of eagles" or refer to their Albanian language, trace their roots to the ancient Illyrians. These ancestors journeyed from central Europe to the Albanian territory around 2000 BCE, living in relative obscurity due to their rugged mountainous terrain and various historical, cultural, and social factors.

Positioned between the Adriatic and Ionian seas, Albania has been a historical bridgehead for conquering nations and empires. The Romans conquered the Illyrians in the 2nd century BCE, and the Byzantine Empire ruled over them from the late 4th century CE. After enduring invasions from various groups, the Albanians fell under Ottoman rule in the

15th century. This lengthy period of Ottoman dominance severed Albania from Western influence. However, by the late 19th century, Albania began distancing itself from the Ottomans, rekindling ties with the West.

Albania declared its independence in 1912, though the great powers of Europe, including Austria-Hungary, Britain, France, Germany, Italy, and Russia, altered its borders, assigning roughly half its land and people to neighboring countries. Between the World Wars, Albania functioned as a monarchy. After World War II, it transformed into a communist state, where the ruling party tightly controlled almost all aspects of life. In the late 20th century, the collapse of communist regimes led to the emergence of new social forces and democratic political parties, aligning with Albania's inclination towards the West and their appreciation of Western culture while preserving their ethnic identity and cultural heritage.

Cultural development in Albania faced challenges during over four decades of communist rule, marked by strict censorship. Subsequent governments have endeavored to promote and preserve the nation's rich cultural traditions. Albania is renowned for its hospitable customs, governed by the "kanun," a set of unwritten laws established by Prince Lekë Dukagjin in the 15th century, regulating various social interactions, including marriage, death, family, and religion. Some Albanians still adhere to these customary laws, including the practice of avenging killings, known as "gjakmarrje" or "blood feuds," which continued in parts of northern Albania into the 21st century.

Daily life in Albania encompasses traditional religious and pagan holidays, along with folk traditions. Agricultural fairs and religious festivals occur year-round, featuring highly skilled sports competitions sometimes held at the national stadium in Tirana. Celebrations like "Dita e Verës" (Spring Day) and folkloric festivals showcase the country's cultural richness. Albania's Independence Day on November 28 is celebrated nationwide.

Albanian cuisine predominantly features meat and seafood dishes such as roasts, biftek (beef loin), qebaps (kabobs), and qoftë (meatballs). Regional specialties like "Fergësë Tirana" and "kukurec" (sheep intestines broiled on a spit) offer diverse flavors. Carp and the rare "koran" (trout) are favored fish. Desserts include "oshaf," a pudding made from figs and sheep's milk. The traditional Albanian drink is "raki," a grape-based brandy typically enjoyed before meals.

Albania boasts a rich heritage of traditional arts, including fine embroidery, lace-making, woodworking, and furniture crafting. Music and storytelling hold a special place in Albanian culture, with epic tales narrated by traditional singers. Albanian folk music, influenced by Turkish and Persian elements, includes iso-polyphony, a form of group singing predominantly performed by men. This unique vocal tradition earned UNESCO recognition as an intangible cultural heritage. Folk instruments like the "çifteli" (a two-stringed mandolin) and the "gërnetë" (a type of clarinet) feature prominently in Albanian music.

Albania also has a strong literary tradition, with renowned contemporary writer Ismail Kadare, whose works have been translated into numerous languages. Early 20th-century poets like Gjergj Fishta, Ndre Mjeda, and Asdren contributed to the country's literary heritage. Fan S. Noli, an Orthodox bishop and brief prime minister, is celebrated for his translations of classic global dramas and poetry at the turn of the 20th century.

## Geography and Climate

Albania shares its borders with Montenegro to the northwest, Kosovo to the northeast,

North Macedonia to the east, and Greece to the southeast and south, while the Adriatic and Ionian seas border it to the west and southwest, respectively. Italy, its close neighbor to the west, is about 50 miles (80 km) away, separated by the Adriatic Sea. The country spans approximately 210 miles (340 km) in length and 95 miles (150 km) in width.

Albania's terrain is mainly mountainous, with roughly three-quarters of its land consisting of mountains and hills rising over 650 feet (200 meters) above sea level. The remaining areas include coastal regions and lowlands. The North Albanian Alps, an extension of the Dinaric Alps, dominate the northern part of the country. These mountains, with peaks nearly reaching

8,900 feet (2,700 meters), are characterized by dense forests and a sparse population.

In contrast, the central mountain region runs from north to south, covering the area from the Drin River to the central Devoll and lower Osum rivers. This region has a higher population density and generally less rugged terrain. In the easternmost part of this region lies Mount Korab, Albania's tallest peak, towering at 9,030 feet (2,752 meters).

South of the central mountain region, you'll find mountain ranges running northwest to southeast, with elevations of up to 8,200 feet (2,500 meters). These ranges, composed of limestone rock, are separated by wide valleys. Unlike the densely forested Alps and the central area, the southern mountains are either bare or sparsely covered with Mediterranean shrubs, oaks, and pines, primarily serving as pasture for livestock.

Stretching along the Adriatic coast for nearly 125 miles (200 km) and extending about 30 miles (50 km) inland are the low and fertile plains of western Albania. This region is crucial for agriculture and industry in the country, and it's also the most densely populated.

## Getting There

Traveling to Albania offers various options, depending on your location, time, and budget.

## By Air

When it comes to flying, Albania's main airport is in Tirana, called Nënë Tereza. You can find direct flights from many European cities, Israel, and Turkey. For travelers from other continents, a layover in a major European city is necessary. There are no direct flights from North America, South America, Africa, or Australia. The closest options for travelers from the Americas are London or Frankfurt. Most flights to Nënë Tereza come from Italy (around 15 cities), followed by German cities. Airlines like British Airways, Lufthansa, Turkish Airlines, and Alitalia operate here. If you prefer low-cost airlines, Wizzair offers flights from Budapest, London, and Dortmund. Another airport, Kukës, is expected to open in 2020 as a low-cost airport.

Getting from Tirana to Nënë Tereza is easy. You can take the shuttle (Rinas Express) from the city center or use a taxi. Bus tickets cost approximately 2€, while taxi fares are around 18€. Make sure to look for the ATEx sign on the taxis, as they are the only approved company at the airport.

**By Ferry**

Ferry travel is a popular way to reach Albania, with most ferries departing from Italy and arriving at Durrës, Vlorë, or Sarandë. Some ferries also come from Greece. Ferries to Durrës depart from Ancona, Bari, and Trieste. If you're in Brindisi, you can catch a ferry to Vlorë and Sarandë. There's also a connection between Sarandë and Corfu in Greece. Renowned Italian ferry operators include Adria Ferries, Adriatica di Navigazione, Azzurra Line, Venezia Lines, and Ilion Lines. For travelers from Greece, consider Sarris and Ionian

Seaways. Prices vary based on the number of passengers, whether you have a vehicle and the time of year.

**By Bus**

Traveling by coach to Albania is another option, although it may not be the most comfortable, it is usually budget-friendly and frequent. Buses to Albania run from Istanbul, Athens, Prishtina, Tetovo, Thessaloniki, Sofia, Larisa, Ohrid, and Ulcinj. Ticket prices range from 10€ to 35€ for a one-way journey, depending on your starting point.

**Getting Around**

Navigating Albania can be a bit challenging, so it's best to stay flexible, be patient, and consider travel information as a helpful hint rather than set in stone.

Most of your travels within the country will likely be by bus. These buses are generally in good condition, fares are budget-friendly, and the roads are gradually getting better. However, it's worth noting that official bus stations are virtually nonexistent. This is less of an issue in smaller towns but can be confusing in a bustling city like Tirana. Additionally, minibusses called "furgons" are sometimes used, although they are technically illegal, especially in larger cities. Nevertheless, some furgons still operate without much interference. They tend to wait until they have enough passengers and may roam around town while doing so.

Albania doesn't have international train connections, but there is a limited rail network. Recently, Tirana's primary train station was relocated to Kashar, a small town near the airport, due to ongoing construction projects in the north of the city. From there, you can find a limited train service to a few destinations within the country.

# Planning Your Trip

## When to visit

The Best time to explore Albania is during the summer season. This is when the weather is usually warm and dry, and it's perfect for enjoying outdoor activities. On the other hand, winters in Albania tend to be relatively mild and wet. While temperatures can differ across various regions, they rarely reach extreme levels. Unlike some of its neighboring countries along the Adriatic and Ionian seas, Albania doesn't experience a massive influx of tourists throughout the year. This makes it an excellent summer destination in Europe, especially if you're looking to enjoy water-based activities.

## Visa and Passport Requirements

Albania, a remarkable country boasting breathtaking natural beauty and captivating destinations, welcomes visitors from around the world. If you're planning to explore Albania and you're not a citizen, you'll need to apply for an Albanian visa.

There are two types of visas to consider based on your intended stay duration:

**1. Short-Term Visa (C):** This visa allows you to spend up to 90 days in Albania within 180 days. It's suitable for various purposes, including:

- Visa for Tourism.
- Visa for Medical visits.

- Visa for Scientific, cultural, sports, and humanitarian activities.
- Visa for Official visits.

**2. Long-Term Visa (D):** The long-term visa grants you a year-long stay in Albania, ideal if you plan to obtain a residence permit. It's issued for purposes such as:
- Student visa.
- Family reunion visa.
- Work visa.
- Diplomatic or service visa.
- Humanitarian or religious activities visa.
- Seasonal employment visa.
- Retirement visa.

When applying for an Albanian visa, you'll need to submit the following required documents:

- A valid passport with a minimum validity of three months beyond your return date. Include any copies of previous visas, if applicable.
- A passport-sized color photo with a plain background.
- Complete and accurate application forms without any missing information.
- Bank statements covering the last six months to demonstrate financial stability during your stay.
- Travel health insurance with a minimum coverage of €30,000 to cover medical expenses while in Albania.
- An invitation letter from a family member or friend in Albania if you're visiting them.

- Proof of accommodation in Albania, which can be a rental agreement, invitation letter, hotel reservation, etc.
- A booked flight itinerary detailing your travel plans, including flight dates, times, airline information, and more.
- For children under 18, a document signed by both parents or legal guardians granting permission for their travel to Albania.

To apply for an Albanian visa, follow these steps:

1. Visit the E-Visa online platform and complete the application.
2. Register or log in to create an account and submit the required documents in PDF format.

3. The Consul will review your application and, if it meets all requirements, will instruct you to proceed with the visa fee payment.

4. Pay the Albania visa fee at the designated bank and attach the payment receipt to your documents.

5. Await a response via text or email from the Consul regarding the status of your visa application, whether it's been approved or denied.

These steps will help make your journey to Albania a smooth and enjoyable one.

**Things to pack**

January

In January, Albania embraces winter, bringing chilly weather with temperatures usually below 10°C and a fair amount of rain. It's not yet time for a seaside dip! Must-haves for January include:
- Raincoat
- Umbrella

- Fleece
- Socks
- Waterproofs
- Warm clothing

February

February brings a glimpse of spring, though beach weather is still a distant dream. The rain persists, and evenings can be chilly, below 10°C. Must-haves for February include:
- Raincoat
- Warm clothing
- Jeans
- Waterproof and comfortable footwear
- Umbrella
- Layers

March

March sees a slight reduction in rain, but evenings remain cool. Temperatures start to rise gradually as the month progresses. Must-haves for March include:
- Sunglasses
- Umbrella
- Jacket
- Jeans and warm clothing
- Layers

April

Spring arrives in April, with delightful days reaching the late teens and early 20s in temperature. Rainfall decreases compared to previous months. Must-haves for April include:
- Light jacket
- Umbrella

- Jeans or pants
- Long dresses for pairing with a jacket
- Sneakers/trainers and ballet pumps for warm days

May

May brings warmer temperatures, but it can still be a bit rainy. Be prepared for occasional showers. Must-haves for May include:

- Sandals and sneakers/trainers
- Umbrella
- Very lightweight jacket
- Shorts
- Dresses

June

June marks the arrival of summer with hot temperatures, even reaching the high 20s.

Don't forget sunscreen, but early June nights can still be comfortably cool. Must-haves for June include:
- Sunscreen
- Sunglasses
- Dresses
- Lightweight pants/linen
- Very light raincoat (just in case)
- Shorts
- Sandals
- Swimwear

July

July is consistently hot, with temperatures in the early 30s. Rain is rare, so take a dip in the sea if you're near it! Must-haves for July include:
- Shorts
- Skirts

- Linen pants
- Sandals
- Sunscreen
- Sunglasses
- Swimwear
- Dresses
- Lightweight clothing in general

August

August is scorching with no rain in sight. Expect the mid to high 30s in temperatures. Beaches are bustling. Must-haves for August include:

- Swimwear
- Sunscreen
- Sunhat
- Sunglasses
- Very light clothing

- Dresses, skirts, shorts, linen pants, etc.
- Sandals

September

September is like an extension of August, slightly cooler as the month progresses. Temperatures average around 30°C, still no rain. Must-haves for September include:
- Swimwear
- Sunscreen
- Sunhat
- Sunglasses
- Sandals, flip flops, etc.
- Skirts, shorts, dresses, lightweight clothing

October

October sees a gentle easing of summer, with daytime temperatures around 23-25°C. Rain increases, especially towards the end of the month. Must-haves for October include:

- Umbrella
- Lightweight rain jacket
- Waterproof sandals or sneakers/trainers
- Sunscreen
- Sunglasses
- Shorts or loose pants
- Dresses
- Light cardigan

November

November heads towards winter, with increasing rain and daytime temperatures

around the low teens. Must-haves for November include:
- Jeans or leggings
- Boots or sneakers/trainers
- Raincoat
- Umbrella
- Warm nightwear
- Waterproof jacket
- Layers

December

December is cold and rainy, with temperatures around 10°C during the day. Expect rain most days and chilly evenings. Must-haves for December include:
- Umbrella
- Waterproof coat
- Warm clothing
- Boots

- Warm socks
- Jeans and long, warm pants

**Tips for staying safe**

Here are some important safety tips for your trip to Albania:

1. Avoid Political Demonstrations: It might be tempting to join a protest or rally, but it's best to steer clear. In 2018, a political protest resulted in injuries to thirteen police officers. Avoid getting caught up in a situation you don't understand, especially if you don't speak the language.

2. Emergency Numbers: Keep these important numbers handy in case of emergencies:
    - Ambulance: 127
    - Police: 129

- Fire: 128

3. Enroll in Safety Programs: If you're from the United States, consider enrolling in the State Department's STEP Program to stay informed about any issues on the ground. Other countries may offer similar programs, so check with your government.

4. Don't Drink and Drive: Albania is known for its wine and raki, but remember that even a small amount of alcohol in your system while driving is illegal and could lead to arrest.

5. Travel Insurance: Get travel insurance and have easy access to your policy information. Share this information with an emergency contact who isn't traveling with you.

6. Keep Your Money Safe: Avoid flaunting cash. Use a mix of credit cards and cash in the city, and keep them securely tucked away. Consider using RFID-protected bags or money belts to prevent theft.

7. Hard Copies of Important Documents: Have hard copies of your card numbers, phone numbers, and passport information in case of theft. Keep copies in different places, like your backpack, or day bag, and email them to yourself.

8. Never Leave Your Belongings Unattended: Avoid leaving your belongings unattended, even in restaurants or cafes. Keep an eye on your items, and if you're in a crowded place, secure your backpack to your chair.

9. Stay Aware of Your Surroundings: Pay attention to your surroundings. Avoid getting engrossed in your phone or wearing headphones while walking alone. Being alert can help you thwart potential thefts.

10. Water Safety: While tap water in major cities like Tirana and Saranda is generally safe, it's best to avoid drinking tap water in rural areas and small towns on the Albanian Riviera. Opt for bottled water or use a water filter.

Remember these tips to ensure a safe and enjoyable trip to Albania.

## Exploring Albania

**Tirana**

Tirana, the lively capital of Albania, brims with history, culture, and natural beauty. Here's a guide to must-see spots and activities that'll make your Tirana trip unforgettable.

**What to Explore:**

1. Skanderbeg Square

At the heart of Tirana lies Skanderbeg Square, named after national hero Gjergj Kastrioti, known as Skanderbeg. This spacious square is surrounded by key government buildings, like the Prime Minister's Office and the National History Museum. Take a leisurely walk, enjoy the fountains, and soak in the lively atmosphere of this central hub.

2. National Museum of Albania

Delve deep into Albania's rich history and heritage at the National Museum of Albania. It houses a vast collection of artifacts, including archaeological finds, historical documents, and art that narrate Albania's story from ancient times to today.

3. Et'hem Bey Mosque

The Et'hem Bey Mosque is a stunning architectural gem, reflecting Tirana's Ottoman history. It's famous for its intricate frescoes and exquisite craftsmanship. Amidst the city's hustle, this mosque offers tranquility, providing a glimpse into Tirana's diverse cultural fabric.

4. Bunk'Art

Step into Albania's Cold War history at Bunk'Art, a one-of-a-kind attraction housed within a former nuclear bunker. Through multimedia exhibits, it sheds light on the country's political history, making for an eye-opening educational experience.

5. Mount Dajti National Park

Escape the city's hustle with a short cable car ride to Mount Dajti National Park. At the mountain's summit, you'll be treated to breathtaking panoramic views of Tirana and its surroundings. Nature lovers, hikers, and those seeking serenity will find it an ideal retreat.

Tirana is a city where the past and present seamlessly blend. From historic sites and museums to vibrant cafes and colorful markets, there's something for everyone in this dynamic city. As you explore Tirana, you'll feel its warmth, resilience, and the genuine hospitality of its people.

So, whether you're into history, culture, or nature, Tirana guarantees a delightful journey full of unique experiences. Take your time to savor Albanian cuisine, connect with locals, and uncover the hidden treasures of this captivating city. Your Tirana adventure awaits!

**Berat and Gjirokastra**

Explore the heart of Albania, where history and captivating architecture await at Berat and Gjirokastra, both UNESCO World Heritage Sites. These ancient cities offer a glimpse into Albania's past, blending centuries-old traditions with stunning landscapes.

**Here's what to discover:**

1. Berati Castle:

In the center of Berat, you'll find its castle, perched on a hill, overlooking the town.

Known as the "City of a Thousand Windows," Berat boasts charming Ottoman-era houses adorned with numerous windows. Inside the castle, you'll encounter winding streets, ancient churches, and panoramic viewpoints with breathtaking views of the town and the Osum River.

2. Onufri Museum:

To explore Albanian art and religious history, don't miss the Onufri Museum. It houses a remarkable collection of icons, artifacts, and religious paintings by the renowned Albanian master, Onufri. The vivid colors and intricate details of these artworks are truly captivating.

3. Gjirokastra Castle:

Gjirokastra, known as the "Stone City," features a well-preserved ancient castle that transports you to another time. Wander through its massive stone walls, dungeons, and towers while enjoying panoramic views of the city and surrounding mountains. Within the castle lies the intriguing Zekate House, showcasing traditional Gjirokastran architecture.

4. Ethnographic Museum:

Immerse yourself in Gjirokastra's culture and daily life at the Ethnographic Museum. Housed in an Ottoman-era building, it displays a wide range of artifacts, including traditional costumes, tools, and household items, offering a vivid glimpse into the region's rural heritage.

Berat and Gjirokastra provide a unique opportunity to step back in time in Albania. With well-preserved architecture, cobblestone streets, and friendly locals, these cities exude an enchanting atmosphere. Don't forget to savor authentic Albanian cuisine at one of the traditional restaurants, where you can soak in the historic ambiance.

As UNESCO World Heritage Sites, Berat and Gjirokastra are not just destinations; they embody Albania's rich cultural heritage. Whether you're a history enthusiast, an architecture lover, or simply seeking a unique travel experience, these cities will leave a lasting impression on your journey through Albania.

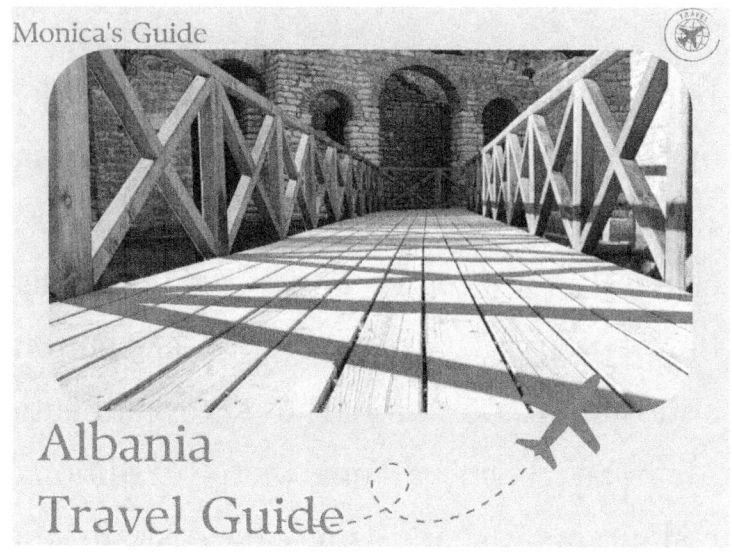

**Butrint**

Located in the southern part of Albania, you'll find the enchanting city of Butrint, designated as a UNESCO World Heritage Site. This hidden gem is a captivating blend of history and nature, offering travelers a unique journey through time.

## Must-See Attractions:

1. The Acropolis

Commence your exploration at the Acropolis, the crown jewel of Butrint. Perched on a hill with stunning views of the Ionian Sea, it reveals the grandeur of the past. As you wander through the ruins, encounter ancient temples, fortifications, and monuments that echo Butrint's Greek, Roman, Byzantine, and Venetian history.

2. The Theater

Transport yourself to antiquity at Butrint's well-preserved theater, constructed during the Roman era. Once a hub for performances and gatherings, it now stands as a testament to the enduring allure of theater, set against lush greenery.

3. The Nymphaeum

The Nymphaeum is a charming sanctuary within Butrint, an ornate Roman structure dedicated to water nymphs. Its intricate carvings and serene ambiance offer a moment for reflection on the city's rich history and natural beauty.

Butrint isn't merely an assortment of ancient ruins; it's a journey through history, where every stone narrates a story. While exploring this archaeological wonder, keep an eye out for the abundant wildlife, including turtles and various bird species, adding an extra layer of charm to your visit.

To fully grasp Butrint's historical significance, consider hiring a knowledgeable local guide. They can provide insights into the city's past and help you uncover its hidden treasures. Enjoy your voyage through Butrint's captivating past and picturesque landscapes.

## The Majestic Albanian Alps

Discover the breathtaking beauty of the Albanian Alps, known as the Accursed Mountains, tucked away in the northern part of Albania. This pristine natural wonderland is a haven for nature lovers and adventurers alike. Two remarkable national parks, Theth National Park and Valbona National Park, await your exploration.

## What to Explore:

Theth National Park:
Venture into the heart of the Albanian Alps and find Theth National Park, a remote and

charming village surrounded by lush valleys, towering peaks, and clear rivers. It's a paradise for hikers, with trails leading to iconic spots like the mesmerizing Blue Eye spring and the culturally significant Lock-in Tower.

Hiking and Biking:
Calling all hiking and biking enthusiasts! The Albanian Alps offer an array of trails suitable for all skill levels. Whether you're an experienced trekker or a casual nature lover, you'll find trails in both Theth and Valbona National Parks that promise stunning vistas and encounters with local flora and fauna.

Valbona National Park:

Adjacent to Theth, Valbona National Park is equally captivating. The Valbona Valley, with its pristine river, dense forests, and charming villages, is a tranquil alpine retreat. Hike through the Valbona Pass for breathtaking panoramas of the surrounding peaks and valleys.

Winter Skiing:

During the winter months, the Albanian Alps transform into a skiing paradise. Explore the region's growing ski resorts for a unique and undiscovered winter sports experience.

Respect the Environment and Communities:

When you visit the Albanian Alps, remember to respect the natural environment and local communities. Many guesthouses and lodges in Theth and Valbona offer warm hospitality and delicious, locally sourced meals, allowing you to immerse yourself in the region's culture while enjoying its natural beauty.

## The Albanian Riviera

The Albanian Riviera, a hidden treasure along the Ionian Sea, invites travelers with its unspoiled beaches, charming coastal towns, and breathtaking scenery. This sun-drenched coastline offers the perfect blend of relaxation and adventure, making it a must-visit destination for beach enthusiasts and culture lovers.

## Explore the Delights

Saranda:

Your journey begins in Saranda, a coastal gem known for its stunning beaches, lively promenades, and ancient sites. Visit the UNESCO-listed Butrint, an ancient city with well-preserved ruins, including a theater, temples, and Roman baths. Enjoy a stroll along the seafront, sip coffee at a seaside café, or embark on a boat tour to the Blue Eye spring and other nearby attractions.

Ksamil:

A short drive from Saranda takes you to Ksamil, a paradise of crystal-clear waters and secluded beaches. Explore the three small islands just offshore, perfect for snorkeling and swimming. Relax on sandy shores, savor fresh seafood at waterfront restaurants, and immerse yourself in the tranquil ambiance of this coastal haven.

Himara:

Further south, Himara offers stunning beaches and a glimpse of Albanian coastal culture. Wander through the old town with its traditional stone houses and cobblestone streets, and savor delicious local cuisine.

Don't miss the panoramic views of the coastline from Himara Castle, a perfect spot for sunset enthusiasts.

Vlora:

Vlora, one of Albania's oldest cities, is a captivating stop on your journey. Explore the Independence Museum, celebrating the nation's liberation from the Ottoman Empire. Take a scenic walk along the waterfront promenade with stunning views of the Adriatic Sea.

Llogara National Park:

Before bidding farewell to the Albanian Riviera, venture into the breathtaking Llogara Pass within Llogara National Park. Whether you drive or hike through this alpine wonderland, you'll be treated to panoramic coastal vistas. It's a photographer's dream and a nature lover's paradise.

The Albanian Riviera promises a diverse range of experiences, from beachfront relaxation to cultural immersion. Whether you're sunbathing on pristine shores, delving into history and culture, or savoring local cuisine, this region ensures a memorable and rejuvenating escape.

As you explore the Albanian Riviera, you'll also have the opportunity to connect with the warm and welcoming locals, enriching your journey with the genuine hospitality of this coastal paradise.

# Food And Drinks

### Traditional Albanian cuisine

**Byrek**

Byrek is Albania's favorite traditional dish, loved for its delicious layers of dough filled with a variety of tasty ingredients. Each Byrek can be a unique culinary experience, with fillings like ricotta cheese, onions, tomatoes, spinach, or meat.

**Tava e Kosit**

Originating from Elbasan and now enjoyed all over Albania, Tava e Kosit is a classic Albanian dish. It features lamb meat, eggs, yogurt, and a blend of herbs, all cooked together in a casserole and baked to perfection.

**Bakllava**

Bakllava is a dessert you can't miss in Albania. Though it has Turkish roots, Albanians have embraced it for centuries. This mouthwatering treat consists of layers of dough filled with nuts and sugar, topped with a sweet syrup called "shërbet." Bakeries across Albania put their spin on Baklava, each with its unique processes, ingredients, and sizes.

## Stuffed Peppers

"Stuffed Peppers" is a beloved Albanian dish, especially popular in the summertime. It consists of peppers filled with a mix of ingredients like ground beef, onions, herbs, and tomato sauce. The specific stuffing can vary depending on the region and the cook's preferences.

## Fergesa

"Fergesa" is a native Albanian dish, commonly found in central Albania, including Tirana. This delightful meal features peppers, tomatoes, onions, cottage cheese, and spices. Once cooked, it turns into a thick and hot dip served in traditional heat-resistant pots. "Fergesa" is both simple and delicious, perfect when paired with bread for a genuine Albanian meal.

## Meatballs

"Meatballs" are highly popular throughout Albania, particularly in local taverns. Locals usually season the meat with spices and mint and serve it with a side salad. One regional variation is "Kernacka," a meatball typical of the Korça plain. This traditional Albanian food pairs well with beverages like beer.

## Shëndetli

"Shëndetli" is a delectable Albanian delicacy, a delightful combination of biscuit and cake textures. Initially, the baked dough has a cookie-like feel, but it transforms into a rich, sweet, and sensational treat. The main ingredients in "Shëndetli" are honey, nuts, eggs, and sugar.

## Petulla

"Petulla" is Albania's authentic take on doughnuts and pancakes, a popular dish in Albanian cuisine. "Petulla" consists of fried dough shaped into fist-sized pieces. You can enjoy them with cheese or drizzle them with honey for a sweet twist.

## Fish in the Oven

Along the Albanian Riviera, local restaurants are supplied with fresh fish and seafood products from the nearby waters. As a small coastal country, Albania keeps its fish recipes simple yet delicious. You can savor freshly caught fish at many places across the country, with oven-cooked fish being a true Mediterranean delight.

## Imam Bajalldi

"Imam Bajalldi" is another Albanian dish with Turkish origins, influenced by centuries of Ottoman Empire occupation. This dish is perfect for summer; it features large eggplants stuffed and baked in the oven. There are numerous variations of the recipe, so the fillings may vary, but most versions include garlic, tomato puree, onions, and parsley.

## Recommend Restaurant

### Oda Restaurant
- Address: Rruga Reshit Çollaku, Tirana

Discover the charm of traditional Albanian cuisine in a historic Ottoman-era house at Oda Restaurant. Feast on delicious dishes like qifqi (rice balls) and tave kosi (yogurt-baked lamb).

**Mullixhiu**

- Address: Rruga Reshit Çollaku, Tirana

Mullixhiu, a Michelin-starred gem in Tirana, offers a modern twist on Albanian flavors. Chef Bledar Kola adds creativity to classic dishes for a unique culinary adventure.

**Mrizi i Zanave**

- Address: Fishte, Lezhë

Mrizi i Zanave, nestled in picturesque countryside, serves farm-to-table delights with a focus on fresh, organic ingredients. Savor traditional Albanian fare with a modern touch.

**Panorama Restaurant**
- Address: Dajti Mountain, Tirana

Panorama Restaurant, atop Dajti Mountain, treats you to stunning Tirana views and mouthwatering Albanian dishes. Indulge in delights like petulla (fried dough) while enjoying the panoramas.

**Korça e Vjetër**

- Address: Rruga Ismail Qemali, Korçë

Korça e Vjetër, a beloved Korçë eatery, serves up traditional dishes from the region. Don't miss their delectable lakror pie and lakror with pumpkin.

## Oda e Junikut

- Address: Gjirokastër Castle, Gjirokastër

Inside Gjirokastër Castle, Oda e Junikut offers a historic ambiance and traditional Albanian cuisine. Sample the local specialty, tave dheu (baked lamb with yogurt and rice).

## Piqni Deli & Bistro

- Address: Rruga Myslym Shyri, Tirana

Piqni Deli & Bistro is renowned for its mouthwatering Albanian meze (appetizers) and modern interpretations of Albanian cuisine. Enjoy an inviting atmosphere and authentic flavors.

**Pëllumbi Restaurant**

- Address: Sheshi Skënderbej, Shkodër

Pëllumbi Restaurant in Shkodër offers a diverse menu featuring both traditional and international dishes. Try their specialties like tave dheu (baked lamb) and koran (trout).

**Ballkoni Dajtit**

- Address: Dajti Mountain, Tirana

Experience a unique dining adventure with breathtaking views at Ballkoni Dajtit, another gem atop Dajti Mountain. Their traditional Albanian dishes are a must-try.

**Restaurant Sergenti**

- Address: Rruga Ismail Qemali, Vlorë

Located in Vlorë, Restaurant Sergenti specializes in fresh seafood and Albanian cuisine. Enjoy a variety of seafood dishes and local flavors by the beautiful Vlorë waterfront.

## *Copyrighted Material*

# Best Places to Visit

### 1. Berat

Berat, often referred to as the "town of a thousand windows," is one of the most captivating cities in the Balkans. The hillside buildings, closely packed with numerous windows, add to its unique charm. History enthusiasts will appreciate the mosques and

Byzantine churches from the Ottoman era scattered throughout the city. Don't miss the 13th-century hilltop castle for breathtaking views. Exploring the city and its two fantastic museums with 16th-century icons and local artifacts is a delightful way to spend your time. To truly appreciate Berat, be sure to view it from the other side of the Osumi River, which offers an incredible perspective.

## 2. Shkodra

Shkodra, located near the vast Lake Skadar, is a charming city renowned for its stunning setting. The impressive Rozafa Castle is a highlight, boasting a rich history ruled by empires like the Illyrians, Venetians, and Ottomans. The castle's massive walls and ruins offer fantastic views of the city and countryside. Shkodra also houses the beautiful Abubakir Mosque and the Orthodox Cathedral, showcasing its historical and architectural heritage. The Historical Museum in the city center is a must-visit, providing insights into the region's history and culture.

### 3. Himare

Himare, with its picturesque coastline and azure waters, is a hidden gem on the Albanian Riviera. It's the perfect destination for a sun-soaked beach vacation. Beyond its serene beachfront boulevard, explore the charming tavernas and Mediterranean atmosphere in the ancient town. Visit the hilltop castle for stunning sea views and venture into the nearby mountains for beautiful trails and panoramic vistas.

Explore the Monastery of the Cross and the Thalia Tisser in the surrounding countryside for a taste of history and architecture. Whether you seek relaxation or cultural and natural exploration, Himare has it all.

## 4. Kruje

Kruje, near Tirana, is the birthplace of Albania's national hero, Gjergj Kastrioti Skanderbeg. Skanderbeg defended Kruje's fortress against the Ottomans for 25 years in the 15th century. The majestic Kruje Castle, perched on the peak above the city, offers breathtaking panoramic views. Visit the 15th-century church and museum dedicated to Skanderbeg, and explore the old bazaar with its charming cafes, restaurants, and diverse shops. The surrounding landscape of serene lakes, valleys, and mountains invites exploration, making Kruje a must-visit destination for its historical sites and beautiful surroundings.

## 5. Tirana

Tirana, Albania's capital, is often the starting point for travelers. While it may not boast many must-see tourist attractions, the 18th-century Et'hem Bey Mosque is a notable exception. The National Historical Museum in Skanderbeg Square is significant, and a monument of Skanderbeg stands in the square's center. Tirana is known for its welcoming people, affordability, and delicious, reasonably-priced food and drinks, making it a convenient and enjoyable stop for travelers exploring Albania's top destinations.

## 6. Explore Butrint National Park

Discover the magic of Albania's Butrint National Park, a unique blend of history and nature that will enchant any visitor. Situated near Greece's Corfu Island, this park is renowned for its remarkable archaeological treasures and diverse ecosystems. Nestled on a peninsula between Lake Butrint and the Vivari Channel, it boasts over 1,200 distinct plant and animal species in its stunning wetlands, hills, and islands. The star attraction here is the awe-inspiring archaeological site, featuring artifacts dating back over 2,500 years, including a Roman theater, Byzantine basilica, castles, and ancient city walls. Strolling through these historical wonders in this picturesque setting is an unforgettable experience. Butrint National Park is a must-visit for treasure seekers exploring Albania.

## 7. Serene Saranda

Nestled in southern Albania, Saranda is a true gem offering breathtaking views of the Ionian Sea, pleasant year-round weather, and a laid-back atmosphere. Despite its coastal development, Saranda's charming streets, diverse restaurants, cozy pubs, and unique gift shops are worth exploring for hours. It serves as an excellent base for further exploration, with the nearby Butrint National Park, a UNESCO World Heritage site with over 2,500 years of history, and the Ksamil Islands, a trio of secluded islands with pristine beaches and crystal-clear waters, just a short boat ride away.

## 8. Gjirokastër's Charm

Gjirokastër, nestled in the south of Albania, is a delightful destination. Its picturesque old town perches atop a scenic valley, boasting winding cobblestone streets lined with quaint homes and historic attractions. More than 500 preserved houses and structures in Gjirokastër are designated as cultural monuments, and the city's distinctive stone rooftops have earned it the nickname "city of stone." Above the charming old bazaar stands Gjirokastër Castle, the second largest castle in the Balkans, featuring captivating walls, ruins, and an underground Cold War bunker. Visitors can also explore the castle's armaments museum.

## 9. Ksamil Islands Oasis

The Albanian Riviera, with its rugged coastline and natural beauty, is a highlight of any Albanian journey. Among its treasures, the Ksamil Islands, a trio of small islands accessible only by boat from Ksamil town, stand out. Part of the Butrint National Park, these islands exemplify Albania's untouched natural beauty. Alongside the islands, the Blue Eye Spring is a natural wonder not to be missed, with its mesmerizingly deep pool of crystal-clear blue water surrounded by lush flora and tranquil surroundings—a must-visit for nature enthusiasts.

## 10. Durrës

Durrës, once the capital of Albania, lies along the country's coastline, not far from Tirana. While it can get busy in the summer, it offers a pleasant beach for both tourists and locals to enjoy. The waterfront boasts numerous restaurants serving delicious fresh seafood. Durrës also presents an abundance of ancient monuments, including the impressive Archaeological Museum and the majestic Roman Amphitheater, both of which have witnessed the city's rich history, marked by battles and influences from various civilizations, such as the Bulgarians, Greeks, Venetians, and Ottomans.

## Accommodation

**Dazzle Coast Resort**

Located in Oricum, the Dazzle Coast Resort is just a stone's throw away from Burrow Beach. Guests can cool off in the seasonal outdoor pool after a sunny day. This five-star hotel also boasts a bar and a private beach area, along with complimentary Wi-Fi for a hassle-free vacation. Prices for rooms at this hotel start at $117 per night.

## Maritime Marina Bay Resort and Casino

With a total of 66 rooms and 24 luxurious suites, the Maritime Marina Bay Resort offers elegantly designed accommodations with all the necessary amenities. The Mediterranean climate allows guests to enjoy their time until evening in the Flora. Prices for rooms at this hotel start at $88 per night.

## Palace Hotel and Spa

Palace Hotel and Spa, located by the breezy sea, even has a private beach area. Guests can enjoy complimentary spa services, including an indoor pool, sauna, hot tubs, and a gym. All rooms and suites are air-conditioned and beautifully furnished, featuring a flat-screen satellite TV, minibar, and comfortable sofa seating. Prices for rooms at this hotel start at $79 per night.

**Gloria Palace Hotel**

Built-in 2008, the Gloria Palace Hotel Royal and Spa is a superior four-star establishment with natural stone architecture and stunning views overlooking Yamador's Beach. It boasts a captivating infinity pool, exclusive rooms, and executive suites. Known for its dedicated service, luxurious surroundings, and breathtaking vistas, it's the most prestigious hotel in the area. The extensive facilities are tastefully designed to convey exclusivity and luxury, making it suitable for romantic getaways or business trips. Prices for rooms at this hotel start at $165 per night.

**Royal G Hotel and Spa**

Situated along the beautiful Adriatic Seacoast, the Royal G Hotel and Spa becomes your new home away from home. Whether you're traveling with a group or your family, their 110 rooms are equipped with everything needed to escape the daily grind. During your stay, you can bask in the sun and sea on the private white sand beach, savor exquisite cuisine in the à la carte restaurant, and unwind in the wellness and spa center. Prices for rooms at this hotel start at $206 per night.

## Clagity Resort and Spa

Welcome to Clagity Resort and Spa! We offer a family-friendly environment with a range of traveler-focused amenities. Our goal is to provide you with a great mix of value, comfort, and convenience. You'll enjoy our 24-hour front desk, currency exchange services, and a sunny terrace. Take a dip in our on-site pool or relax in the lounge. Accommodation rates at this hotel begin at just $93 per night.

## La Brisa Boutique Hotel

Discover the enchanting turquoise coastline of the Ionian Sea at La Brisa Boutique Hotel. Nestled in one of the most beautiful villages on the Albanian Riviera, our hotel is an oasis of elegance and charm. Located along the main sea promenade, our modern and unique architecture makes us your top choice for rejuvenating your body and soul. Accommodation rates at this hotel start at $78 per night.

**Prado Luxury Hotel**

Indulge in your private paradise at Prado Luxury Hotel, situated on the stunning Ionian Sea. With pristine turquoise waters and sandy beaches, this beachfront resort offers newly furnished guest rooms and suites, a lavish spa, and a wide range of activities. All this comes with the warm and welcoming Albanian hospitality. Accommodation rates at this hotel begin at $565 per night.

## Rare Boutique Hotel

Rare Boutique Hotel, located in Himare just steps from Spiel Beach, offers modern luxury and gracious hospitality. Experience five-star comfort with air-conditioned rooms equipped with essential amenities like a desk, kettle, fridge, safe, flat-screen TV, and a private balcony with a shower. Enjoy breathtaking sea views from your room. Accommodation rates start at $76 per night.

## Melia Durres Albania

At Melia Durres Albania, every detail is designed to make your stay unforgettable on the Albanian Coast. Discover exceptional facilities and exclusive services. Our designer rooms with avant-garde decor are fully equipped to ensure a memorable experience. Additionally, the hotel features six restaurants and bars to enhance your vacation. Accommodation rates at this hotel start at $119 per night.

# Practical Information

### Exploring the Local Language

When you travel, connecting with the local culture is a fantastic part of the experience, and language plays a big role. While Albanian is the official language of Albania, you'll often hear English spoken, especially in cities. However, showing an interest in the local language is always appreciated. Here, we've got some handy Albanian phrases and tips to help you bridge any language gaps during your Albania adventure.

## Albanian Language Essentials:

1. Hello:
   - Albanian: Tungjatjeta (toon-jat-yet-a)

A friendly way to kick off any conversation.

2. Goodbye:
   - Albanian: Mirupafshim (meer-oo-paf-shcem)

Use this when it's time to part ways.

3. Thank you:
   - Albanian: Faleminderit (fa-lay-min-deh-reet)

Express your gratitude with this common phrase.

4. Yes:
   - Albanian: Po (poh)

A straightforward way to agree.

5. No:
- Albanian: Jo (yoh)

The simple way to say no.

6. Excuse me / I'm sorry:
- Albanian: Më fal (muh fal)

Employ this when you need someone's attention or want to apologize.

7. Please:
- Albanian: Ju lutem (yoo loo-tem)

A polite way to make requests.

8. Do you speak English?:
- Albanian: A flisni anglisht? (ah flees-nee ahn-gleesht?)

Handy when you need to switch to English.

Feel free to use these phrases to enhance your travel experience in Albania!

## Tips for Travelers

1. Learn Some Albanian Phrases: While many Albanians speak English, picking up a few basic Albanian phrases can make a positive impression and help in everyday situations.

2. Use Gestures: When language is a barrier, employing gestures and simple drawings can be a fun and effective way to get your message across.

3. Leverage Translation Apps: Keep a smartphone with a translation app handy to swiftly translate words and phrases while on the go.

4. Seek Local Assistance: Albanians are generally friendly and ready to assist travelers. Don't hesitate to ask for directions or recommendations.

5. Show Respect for Local Culture: Politeness and respect for local customs are universally appreciated. Even if you're not fluent in the language, a friendly and respectful attitude goes a long way.

6. Embrace Local Dining: In Albanian restaurants, you can often point to menu items or use photos to order if you're unsure about pronunciation. Enjoy local cuisine like a pro!

## Shopping

Shopping in Albania offers a unique blend of traditional bazaars, modern malls, and artisanal markets. Whether you seek souvenirs, local crafts, or the latest fashion, this chapter will be your guide.

**Traditional Markets:**

1. Bazaars: In cities like Tirana and Shkodër, vibrant bazaars bustle with local vendors offering fresh produce, clothing, and household goods, providing a glimpse into daily Albanian life.

2. Korca Bazaar (Pazari i Vjetër): Situated in the heart of Korçë, this historic bazaar is a must-visit for traditional Albanian crafts, including handmade carpets, textiles, honey, and sweets.

3. Kruja Bazaar (Pazari i Krujës): Kruja's bazaar is famous for its skilled artisans crafting traditional Albanian clothing, jewelry, and souvenirs. Feel free to negotiate prices here.

**Souvenirs:**

1. Traditional Clothing: Albanian clothing, like embroidered blouses and vests, makes for a popular souvenir. Seek boutiques and markets for these exquisite garments.

2. Crafts and Artwork: Handcrafted items such as wooden carvings, ceramics, and paintings can be found in local markets and galleries. Look for pieces that capture Albanian culture.

3. Filigree Jewelry: Albania is renowned for its intricate filigree jewelry, often featuring symbolic motifs. Gjirokastër is an excellent spot for shopping for these exquisite pieces.

## Shopping Malls:

1. Toptani Shopping Center (Tirana East Gate): Located in the capital, Tirana, this modern mall offers a mix of international and local brands, perfect for fashion and electronics shopping.

2. QTU Shopping Center (Tirana Ring Center): Another popular mall in Tirana, it houses a variety of shops, a food court, and family-friendly entertainment.

3. City Park (Parku i Qytetit - Tirana): This large shopping and entertainment complex in Tirana boasts numerous shops, cafes, and restaurants, making it ideal for a day of shopping and leisure.

## Shopping Tips:

Currency: The official currency is the Albanian Lek (ALL), so carry cash for smaller purchases. Credit cards are widely accepted in larger stores and malls.

Haggling: Bargaining is common in traditional markets, so negotiate prices respectfully and with a smile.

Opening Hours: Most shops open around 9:00 AM, close for a siesta in the afternoon, and reopen late afternoon, closing around 8:00 PM. Malls have longer hours.

Tax-Free Shopping: Keep an eye out for the "Tax-Free" sign, allowing tourists to receive a refund of Value Added Tax (VAT) on certain purchases.

## Emergency

When you're on the go, it's essential to be ready for unexpected situations. This chapter offers advice on handling emergencies in Albania, such as medical issues, accidents, and getting in touch with the right authorities.

### Medical Emergencies:

1. Dial 127: If there's a medical emergency, call 127, the emergency medical services hotline. While the operators usually speak Albanian, it's wise to have someone who speaks the language assist you if necessary.

2. Medical Facilities:

Albania has hospitals and medical centers across the country. In cities like Tirana, you'll find well-equipped hospitals with English-speaking medical staff. Some recommended hospitals are:

- Mother Teresa Hospital: Rruga e Dibrës, Tirana
- American Hospital Tirana: Rruga e Bogdaneve, Tirana

3. Travel Insurance:

Before you travel, make sure you have comprehensive travel insurance covering medical emergencies. Keep a copy of your insurance policy and contact details with you at all times.

**Police and Law Enforcement:**

1. Dial 129: If you encounter criminal activity, an accident, or require police assistance, dial 129 for emergency police services.

2. Tourist Police: Major tourist areas have Tourist Police who can assist tourists in various languages. They offer guidance and support for issues like theft or lost documents.

**Natural Disasters:**

1. Earthquakes: Albania is prone to earthquakes. If you experience one, remember to drop, cover, and hold on. Follow local authorities' instructions and be ready for aftershocks.

2. Weather-Related Emergencies: During extreme weather conditions, like flooding or

storms, stay updated through local news and heed local authorities' advice.

**Lost or Stolen Documents:**

1. Report to the Police: If you lose your passport, ID, or other vital documents, report it to the police immediately. A police report is necessary for replacing documents.

2. Embassy or Consulate: Contact your home country's embassy or consulate in Tirana for assistance with replacing lost or stolen documents. They can guide you through the required steps.

**General Safety Tips:**

Emergency Numbers: Save important emergency numbers in your phone and jot them down in case your phone is lost or not working.

Travel Companions: It's safer to travel with a group or at least one other person, especially in remote areas.

Local Contacts: Keep contact information for your accommodations and local contacts readily available.

Language Barrier: While many Albanians understand basic English, having a translation app or phrasebook can be handy for emergency communication.

Stay Informed: Stay updated with local news and government advisories, particularly in regions prone to natural disasters or civil unrest.

Emergencies can be unsettling, but with proper preparation and knowledge of local resources, you can reduce their impact and ensure a safer journey in Albania. Always prioritize your safety and well-being, and don't hesitate to seek assistance when needed.

# Your 5 Days Itinerary

**DAY 1**

Discovering the Capital City

MORNING

Kick off your day with a scrumptious breakfast at Tiffany, a well-loved café famous for its pastries and coffee. Next, head to Skanderbeg Square (Sheshi

Skënderbej), Tirana's main square, and admire the Skanderbeg Monument. Take a relaxed stroll around the square to soak up the city's lively vibes.

AFTERNOON

For lunch, make your way to Oda Restaurant, a traditional Albanian eatery in the heart of Tirana. Relish authentic Albanian cuisine and savor dishes like Byrek and Tavë Kosi. Then, explore the Tirana National Historical Museum (Muzeu Historik Kombëtar) to delve into Albania's rich history and culture.

EVENING

As the evening sets in, ascend the Tirana Clock Tower (Kulla e Sahatit) for breathtaking panoramic views of the city at sunset. Afterward, dine at Sespira Lounge, a rooftop restaurant with a stunning view of Tirana's skyline. Savor a delectable meal while gazing at the city lights.

BEDTIME

Rest up. Discover great accommodations in Tirana.

**DAY 2**

Nature and Culture

MORNING

Begin your day with a visit to the Dajti Express Cable Car (Dajti Ekspres). Take a scenic cable car ride to the summit of Mount Dajti and relish awe-inspiring views of Tirana and the surrounding landscapes.

Explore hiking trails and breathe in the fresh mountain air.

AFTERNOON

For lunch, dine at Kalemi, a cozy restaurant near the cable car station. Enjoy traditional Albanian dishes crafted with fresh local ingredients. Later, visit the Et'hem Bey Mosque (Xhamia e Et'hem Beut), known for its remarkable architecture and intricate frescoes.

EVENING

In the evening, explore the Pyramid of Tirana (Enver Hoxha Pyramid), a distinctive architectural landmark. Then, indulge in dinner at Bordo Restaurant, a trendy spot celebrated for modern Albanian cuisine. Savor a delightful meal in an elegant setting.

BEDTIME

Rest up. Find excellent accommodations in Tirana.

**DAY 3**

Exploring the Historic City

MORNING

Embark on a day trip to Krujë, a historic city just outside Tirana. Begin your day by visiting the Krujë Castle (Kalaja e Krujës), a medieval fortress offering sweeping views of the city and the nearby mountains. Explore the castle grounds and learn about Albania's history.

## AFTERNOON

Lunchtime calls for a visit to Rozafa Restaurant, a traditional Albanian eatery near the castle. Enjoy authentic Albanian dishes while taking in the stunning city views. Afterward, explore the Skanderbeg Museum within the castle to delve deeper into the story of the national hero, Skanderbeg.

## EVENING

As evening falls, wander the narrow streets of Krujë's old bazaar. Explore local shops and browse for traditional Albanian crafts and souvenirs. For dinner, experience Trattoria Romantica, a charming Italian restaurant nestled in the heart of the old town. Relish delicious Italian cuisine in a romantic setting.

BEDTIME

Rest up. Find excellent accommodations in Krujë.

## DAY 4

Beaches and History

MORNING

Embark on a day trip to Durrës, a coastal city renowned for its beautiful beaches and ancient ruins. Start your day by exploring the Durrës Amphitheatre, one of the largest Roman amphitheaters in the Balkans. Delve into the city's Roman history as you wander through the ruins.

## AFTERNOON

For lunch, head to Vila Verde, a beachfront restaurant famous for its fresh seafood and Mediterranean cuisine. Savor a delectable meal with a view of the sea. Afterward, relax on the sandy beaches of Durrës and take a refreshing dip in the Adriatic Sea.

EVENING

In the evening, visit the Durrës Archaeological Museum, located near the city center. Explore the museum's collection of ancient artifacts and learn about Durrës' history. For dinner, try Amor, a popular restaurant celebrated for its fusion of Italian and Albanian cuisine. Enjoy a romantic seaside dinner.

BEDTIME

Rest up. Find excellent accommodations in Durrës.

## DAY 5

Hidden Gems and Natural Wonders

MORNING

Commence your day with a visit to the Cave of Pëllumbas (Shpella e Pëllumbasit), a hidden treasure just outside Tirana. Explore the underground caves and marvel at the stalactites and stalagmites. Afterward, relish a picnic lunch in the stunning natural surroundings.

AFTERNOON

After lunch, visit the Pristina Ethnographic Museum (Muzeu Etnologjik), nestled in the heart of Tirana. Learn about Albania's traditional culture and customs through the museum's exhibits. Later, take a stroll in

Tirana's Grand Park, enjoying the lush greenery and fresh air.

EVENING

In the evening, unwind at Garden Food & Bar, a trendy outdoor bar in the Blloku neighborhood. Sip on a refreshing cocktail or savor a glass of local wine in a relaxed atmosphere. For dinner, indulge in Saranda Aquarium, a seafood restaurant known for its fresh fish and seafood dishes. Enjoy a mouthwatering meal before returning to your hotel.

BEDTIME

Rest up. Find excellent accommodations in Tirana.

## Conclusion

As we wrap up our journey in this incredible country, I hope you've grown to love Albania's varied landscapes, vibrant culture, and the warmth of its people.

From the lively streets of Tirana to the serene Albanian Riviera, we've explored the very best of what this nation offers. Albania's unique mix of ancient history, Ottoman influences, and modern vitality weaves a tapestry of experiences you won't forget.

As you get ready to say goodbye to this captivating land, I invite you to delve deeper into the Albanian way of life. Go off the beaten path to discover hidden villages, unspoiled beaches, and charming mountain towns. Immerse yourself in local traditions, savor delicious Albanian cuisine, and embrace the hospitality of the Albanian people.

Remember, travel isn't just about the destinations; it's about the memories you create. Albania has a special way of capturing the hearts of those who explore it. Whether you come for its rich history, breathtaking scenery, or the thrill of the unknown, Albania welcomes you with open arms.

As you embark on your Albanian adventure, may you find inspiration, wonder, and a profound appreciation for the beauty and diversity that make this country truly unique. Safe travels, and may your journey be as unforgettable as Albania itself.

Faleminderit dhe mirupafshim! (Thank you and goodbye!)

# ALBANIA
## Travel Planner

This Travel journal belongs to:
_____

Contact Address:
_____
_____
_____

# Travel Itinerary

Budget ....................................

Activity

Hotel Details

Flight Departure

Flight Arrival

# My Destination

# Packing List

# Packing List

# Packing List

# My Notes

# My Notes

# My Notes

# My Notes

------------------------------------------------

------------------------------------------------

------------------------------------------------

------------------------------------------------

------------------------------------------------

------------------------------------------------

------------------------------------------------

------------------------------------------------

# My Notes

----------------------------------------

----------------------------------------

----------------------------------------

----------------------------------------

----------------------------------------

----------------------------------------

----------------------------------------

----------------------------------------

# My Notes

---------------------------------------------------

---------------------------------------------------

---------------------------------------------------

---------------------------------------------------

---------------------------------------------------

---------------------------------------------------

---------------------------------------------------

---------------------------------------------------

# My Notes

# My Notes

----------------------------------------

----------------------------------------

----------------------------------------

----------------------------------------

----------------------------------------

----------------------------------------

----------------------------------------

----------------------------------------

# My Notes

# My Notes

# My Notes

# My Notes

# My Notes

Printed in Great Britain
by Amazon

45734639R00079